EDMUND HILLARY

REACHES THE TOP OF EVEREST

By Nel Yomtov

Illustration By Samir Barrett and Dave Wheeler
Color By Gerardo Sandoval

BELLWETHER MEDIA • MINNEAPOLIS, MN

STRAY FROM REGULAR READS WITH BLACK SHEEP BOOKS. FEEL A RUSH WITH EVERY READ!

Library of Congress Cataloging-in-Publication Data

Yomtov, Nelson.
  Edmund Hillary Reaches the Top of Everest / by Nel Yomtov.
      pages cm. -- (Black Sheep: Extraordinary Explorers)
   Summary: "Exciting illustrations follow the events of Edmund Hillary reaching the top of Mount Everest. The combination of brightly colored panels and leveled text is intended for students in grades 3 through 7"-- Provided by publisher.
   Audience: Ages 7 to 12
   In graphic novel form.
   Includes bibliographical references and index.
   ISBN 978-1-62617-291-3 (hardcover: alk. paper)
   1. Hillary, Edmund, 1919-2008--Juvenile literature. 2. Mountaineers--New Zealand--Biography--Juvenile literature. 3. Mountaineering expeditions--Everest, Mount (China and Nepal)--History--Juvenile literature. 4. Everest, Mount (China and Nepal)--Description and travel--Juvenile literature. I. Title.
   GV199.92.H54Y66 2016
   796.522095496--dc23
                                        2014050315

This edition first published in 2016 by Bellwether Media, Inc.

No part of this publication may be reproduced in whole or in part without written permission of the publisher. For information regarding permission, write to Bellwether Media, Inc., Attention: Permissions Department, 5357 Penn Avenue South, Minneapolis, MN 55419.

Text copyright © 2016 by Bellwether Media, Inc. BLACK SHEEP and associated logos are trademarks and/or registered trademarks of Bellwether Media, Inc.

SCHOLASTIC, CHILDREN'S PRESS, and associated logos are trademarks and/or registered trademarks of Scholastic Inc.

Printed in the United States of America, North Mankato, MN.

Table of Contents

A Lofty Goal	4
The Climb Begins	6
The Final Assault	14
On Top of the World!	18
More About Edmund and Everest	22
Glossary	23
To Learn More	24
Index	24

Orange text identifies *historical quotes*.

May 7, 1953: Colonel Hunt gathers his team to plan the **assault** on the summit.

"First, we have to climb the Lhotse Face and establish a camp on the South **Col**. Then we have to set up a higher camp."

"We'll make two assaults. The first climbing team will be Charles Evans and Tom Bourdillon. If they don't make it, Edmund and Tenzing will try."

More About Edmund and Everest

- The expedition traveled with about 10,000 pounds (4,500 kilograms) of equipment and supplies.

- In 1951, Edmund was part of an unsuccessful expedition to climb Everest.

- Edmund climbed ten other tall peaks in the Himalayas after conquering Everest. He also took part in a successful expedition to the South Pole in 1958.

- More than 4,000 people have climbed Mount Everest since Edmund and Tenzing did it in 1953.

- At 29,035 feet (8,850 meters) high, Mount Everest is as tall as about 23 Empire State Buildings stacked on top of each other.

- Tibetans call Mount Everest *Chomolungma*, which means "Goddess Mother of the World." Nepalese people call it *Sagarmatha*, meaning "Ocean Mother."

- Junko Tabei of Japan was the first woman to reach the summit of Mount Everest. She accomplished this on May 16, 1975.

Glossary

altitude—the height of something above the ground or sea level; it is harder to breathe at higher altitudes.

assault—an attempt to reach the summit of a mountain

avalanche—large masses of falling snow, ice, and rock

base—the bottom or lowest part of the mountain

base camp—the lowest camp from which an expedition sets out

col—the lowest point of a ridge between two peaks

colonel—a high-ranking officer in the armed forces

crevasse—a deep crack in a glacier

cwm—a steep-walled basin on a mountain at the end of a valley

descent—a downward movement

expedition—a long trip made for a specific purpose

icefall—an area of loose ice that looks like a frozen waterfall

knights—gives a high honor

porters—people who carry equipment on an expedition

ridge—a long, narrow strip of land on top of a mountain

Sherpa—a member of a Tibetan people living on the southern slopes of the Himalayas in eastern Nepal

summit—the highest point of a mountain

To Learn More

At the Library

Bodden, Valerie. *To the Top of Mount Everest*. Mankato, Minn.: Creative Education, 2012.

Helfand, Lewis. *Conquering Everest: The Lives of Edmund Hillary and Tenzing Norgay*. New Delhi, India: Campfire, 2011.

Sydelle, Kramer. *To the Top!: Climbing the World's Highest Mountain*. New York, N.Y.: Random House, 2003.

On the Web

Learning more about Edmund and Everest is as easy as 1, 2, 3.

1. Go to www.factsurfer.com.
2. Enter "Edmund and Everest" into the search box.
3. Click the "Surf" button and you will see a list of related web sites.

With factsurfer.com, finding more information is just a click away.

Index

Bourdillon, Tom, 9, 11, 12
camps, 5, 6, 7, 8, 9, 10, 11, 12, 14, 15, 21
crevasse, 6, 7, 17
Elizabeth II (queen), 21
Evans, Charles, 9, 11, 12
Great Britain, 20
historical quotes, 13, 16, 18
Hunt, John (colonel), 4, 7, 9, 11, 13, 14, 20
icefall, 5, 6, 7
India, 20
Lhotse Face, 5, 9, 10
Mount Everest, 4, 5, 10, 12, 16, 20
Nepal, 4, 20
Norgay, Tenzing, 5, 8, 9, 10, 11, 12, 13, 14, 15, 16, 17, 19, 20, 21
Sherpa, 5, 11
South Col, 5, 9, 11, 21
summit, 4, 5, 9, 13, 17, 20
United Nations, 20
Western Cwm, 5, 7, 8, 10